MARK McGWIRE
THE HOME RUN KING

Rob Kirkpatrick

The Rosen Publishing Group's
PowerKids Press™

Published in 2001 by The Rosen Publishing Group, Inc.
29 East 21st Street, New York, NY 10010

First Edition

Book Design: Michael de Guzman

Photo Credits: p. 4 © Rob Tringali Jr./SportsChrome; p. 7 © Steve Woltman/SportsChrome and CORBIS-Bettmann; p. 8 Courtesy of USC Sports Information Department; p. 11 Courtesy of Tacoma Rainiers; p. 12 © SportsChrome; p. 15 © Otto Creule/Allsport; p. 16 © AP Wide World; p. 19 © Elsa Hasch/Allsport and © SportsChrome; p. 20 © Vince Laforet/Allsport; p. 22 © Elsa Hasch/Allsport.

Kirkpatrick, Rob.
        Mark McGwire / by Rob Kirkpatrick.
          p. cm — (Great record breakers in sports)
        Includes index.
        Summary: A brief biography of the Cardinals' first baseman who broke Roger Maris's home run record by hitting 70 homers in 1998.
        ISBN 0-8239-5630-X (lib. bdg)
        1. McGwire, Mark, 1963—Juvenile literature. 2. Baseball players—United States—Biography—Juvenile literature. [1. McGwire, Mark, 1963- 2. Baseball players.] I. Title. II. Series.

GV865.M396 K568 2000
796.357'092—dc21
[B]
                                                                                                99-042490

Manufactured in the United States of America

CONTENTS

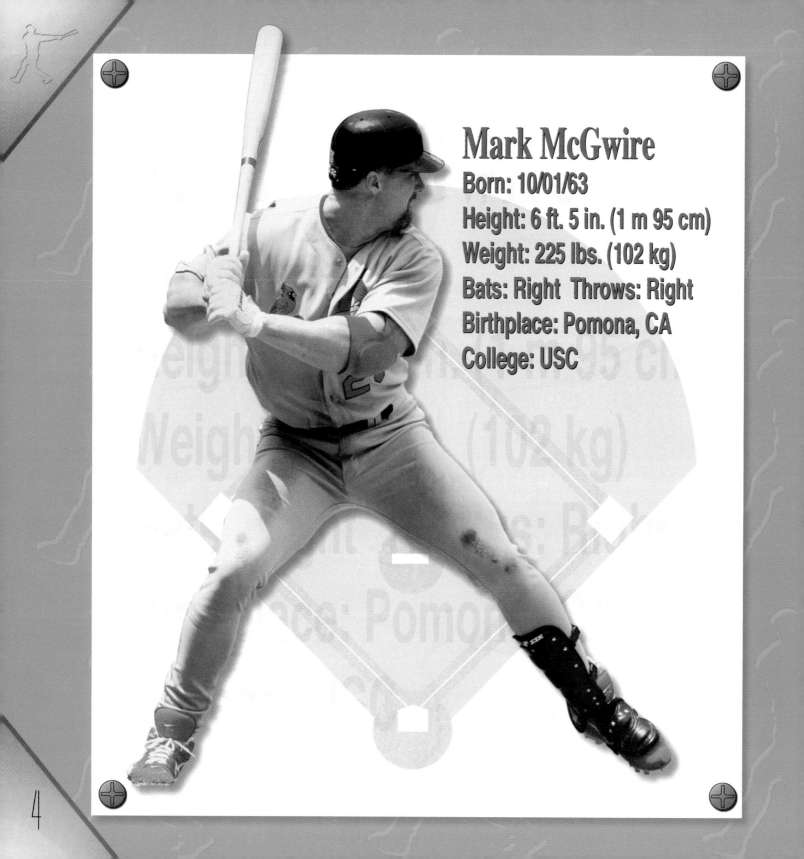

Mark McGwire
Born: 10/01/63
Height: 6 ft. 5 in. (1 m 95 cm)
Weight: 225 lbs. (102 kg)
Bats: Right **Throws:** Right
Birthplace: Pomona, CA
College: USC

THE HOME RUN

In 1998, Mark McGwire hit more home runs than any baseball player has ever hit in one season. A home run is when the batter hits the ball over the **outfield** fence and gets to run around the **bases**. Home runs score points for the team. Mark McGwire is one of the most **popular** baseball players today because he hits a lot of home runs. In 1998, he hit 70 home runs. Now Mark holds the **record** for hitting the most home runs in one season.

◀ *Sports fans are interested in information like where Mark McGwire was born or where he went to school.*

STATISTICS IN BASEBALL

Baseball **statistics**, or "stats," have been recorded since 1876. Stats let us compare today's players to players from the past. For example, in 1876, a player named George Hall held the record for home runs, even though he hit only five! Players hit fewer home runs back then because teams only played 60 or 70 games per season. In 1927, when teams played 154 games per season, Babe Ruth set a new record with 60 home runs. Then, in 1961, Roger Maris hit 61 home runs in 162 games. Today, each team plays 162 games per season. Players have more chances to hit home runs. Mark's home run record helps us see how baseball has changed over the years.

All of these baseball players have become a part of baseball history by holding the home run record.

Mark McGwire
70 Home Runs in 1998

Roger Maris
61 Home Runs in 1961

Roger Maris

Babe Ruth
60 Home Runs in 1927

Babe Ruth

George Hall
5 Home Runs in 1876

George Hall

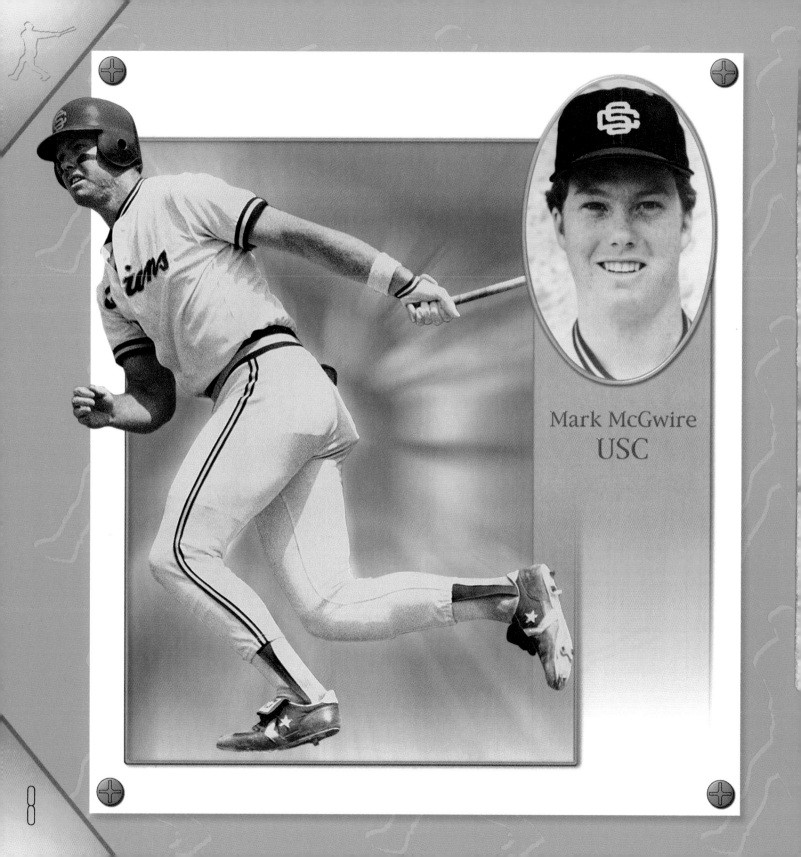

Mark McGwire
USC

8

MARK ALWAYS LIKED BASEBALL

Mark grew up in California. His family used to take him to watch the California Angels play. He played Little League, a baseball league for children, when he was young. The first ball he hit was a home run! Mark played the position of **pitcher** on his high school team. In fact, he was such a good pitcher that when someone from the Montreal Expos, a **professional** baseball team, saw him play, they asked him to join their team. Mark wanted to go to **college** instead. The University of Southern California, or USC, wanted Mark to pitch for them, too. They let him go to school for free so he would join their team. This way Mark could go to college and keep playing baseball.

◀ *The team Mark played on in college was called the Trojans.*

MARK CHANGES POSITIONS AND GOES PRO

Pitching is hard on the player's arm, so pitchers need to rest after a game. Since he was usually pitching, Mark did not get to hit very much in his first year at USC. The next year, Mark switched to first base. This way he could hit every day. In fact, he hit 32 home runs in his junior year at USC in 1984. That was more home runs than any other college player had hit that year. A professional team called the Oakland A's asked Mark to play for them. He agreed. In 1984, he left college and played in the Oakland A's **minor league** system until 1986. This gave him some time to practice hitting against professional pitchers. Soon he was ready for the **major leagues**.

Mark played on one of the teams in the A's minor league system. The team was called the Tacoma Tigers. ▶

25 Mark McGwire
First Baseman

*1987 AL Rookie of the Year
AL Home Run Champion

Number of Home Runs

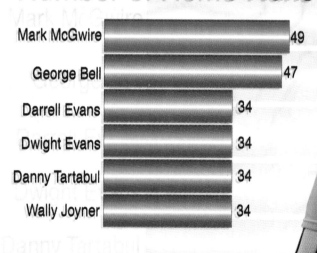

Player	Home Runs
Mark McGwire	49
George Bell	47
Darrell Evans	34
Dwight Evans	34
Danny Tartabul	34
Wally Joyner	34

* AL (American League)

A BIG HIT IN THE BIG LEAGUES

In 1987, the Oakland A's decided Mark was good enough to be their full-time first baseman. Mark was a **rookie** that season. Rookies are new major league players. Sometimes rookies have a hard time getting used to playing in the major leagues. This is because all of the players are so good. The people he played against that year were very good, but Mark was good, too. He hit a lot of home runs for the A's. By the end of the season, he had hit 49 home runs. That was more than any rookie had ever hit in the history of baseball. He set the rookie home run record!

◀ *There were a lot of good hitters starting out in the American League in 1987, but Mark was the best.*

MARK AND THE A'S WIN IT ALL!

Baseball is a team sport. This means that many players must work together to help their team win games. Mark helped the A's win a lot of games. In 1988, the A's won so many games that they got to play in the **World Series**. They played against the Los Angeles Dodgers. Mark helped the A's win one game by hitting a home run, but the Dodgers won the series anyway. Mark's team was disappointed, but they did not give up. In 1989, they went to the World Series again, and this time they won. Mark did not hit any home runs in this series, but he was still happy. Mark's team had won the championship!

The Oakland A's won the 1989 World Series 4 games to 0. ▶

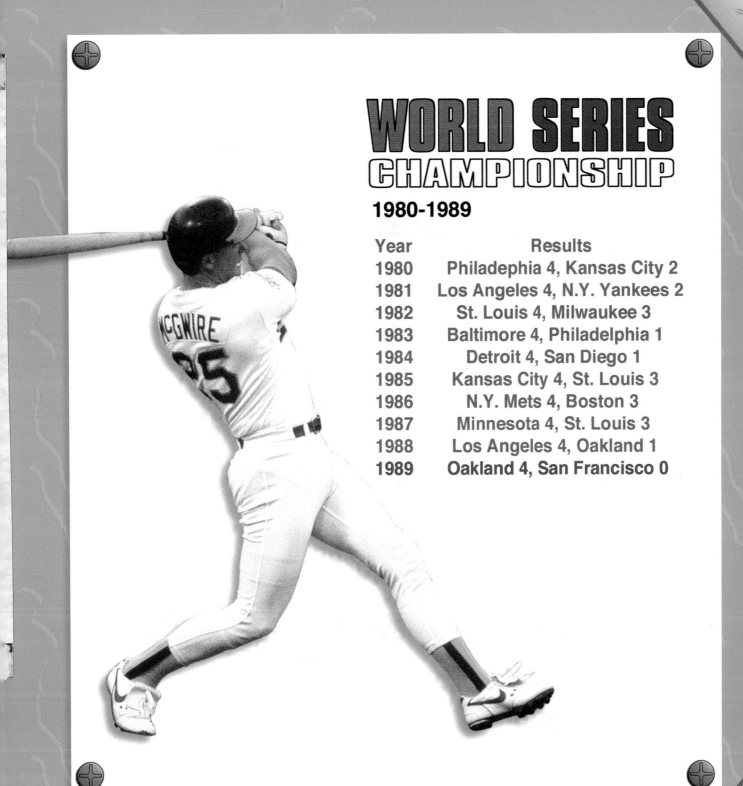

WORLD SERIES CHAMPIONSHIP

1980-1989

Year	Results
1980	Philadephia 4, Kansas City 2
1981	Los Angeles 4, N.Y. Yankees 2
1982	St. Louis 4, Milwaukee 3
1983	Baltimore 4, Philadelphia 1
1984	Detroit 4, San Diego 1
1985	Kansas City 4, St. Louis 3
1986	N.Y. Mets 4, Boston 3
1987	Minnesota 4, St. Louis 3
1988	Los Angeles 4, Oakland 1
1989	Oakland 4, San Francisco 0

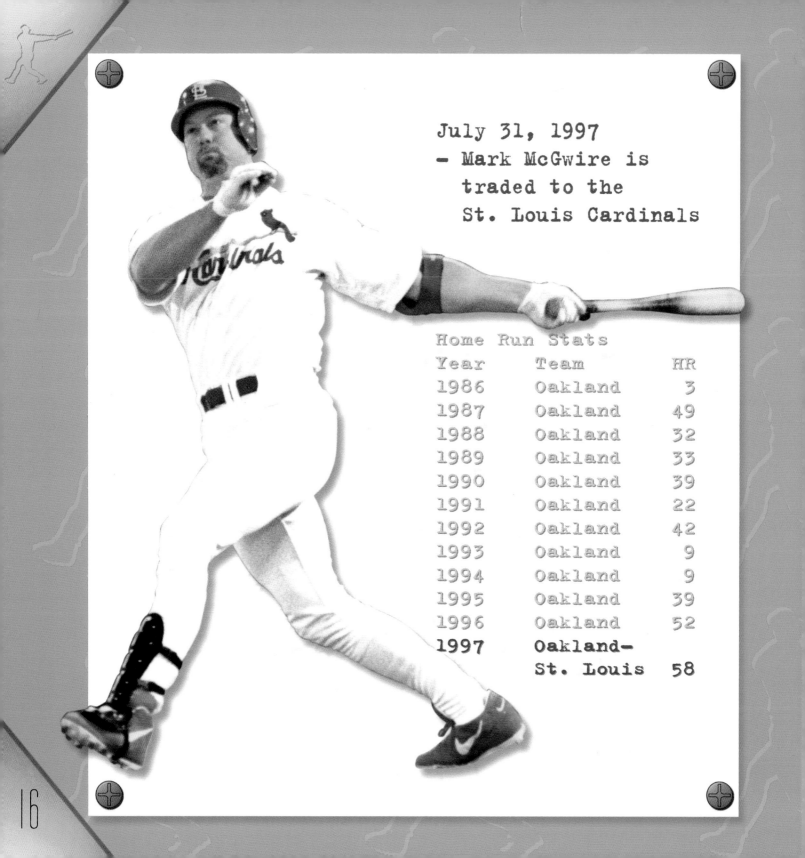

July 31, 1997
- Mark McGwire is
  traded to the
  St. Louis Cardinals

Home Run Stats

Year	Team	HR
1986	Oakland	3
1987	Oakland	49
1988	Oakland	32
1989	Oakland	33
1990	Oakland	39
1991	Oakland	22
1992	Oakland	42
1993	Oakland	9
1994	Oakland	9
1995	Oakland	39
1996	Oakland	52
1997	Oakland–St. Louis	58

MARK MOVES TO ST. LOUIS

Mark kept working on his **swing**, and he became an even better hitter. In 1996, Mark hit 52 home runs. The A's did not win many games, though, and some fans stopped coming to see the team play. When fans stopped coming the A's started losing money. They could not afford to pay Mark anymore. In the middle of the 1997 season, they **traded** Mark to the St. Louis Cardinals. Mark had already hit 34 home runs that season for the A's. Mark hit a lot of home runs for the Cardinals, too. He hit 24 home runs for the Cardinals in less than half a season. Cardinals fans were excited to have Mark hitting for their favorite team.

◀ *Mark hit 58 home runs the year he was traded to the St. Louis Cardinals.*

THE GREAT HOME RUN RACE

In 1998, Mark McGwire and another baseball player named Sammy Sosa had what people called the great home run race. Sammy is an outfielder for the Chicago Cubs. Both Mark and Sammy hit a lot of home runs early in the season. Mark became the first player ever to hit 50 or more home runs three seasons in a row. At the end of August, both Mark and Sammy had hit 55 home runs each. They both seemed like they would break Roger Maris's record of 61 home runs. Fans wondered who would hit the most home runs. More people started watching baseball in 1998 because it was so thrilling to watch Mark and Sammy hit home runs.

Mark and Sammy Sosa had both hit 55 home runs by August 31, 1998. ▶

1998 Home Run Race
(through August 31)

Mark McGwire ▬▬▬▬ 55
Sammy Sosa ▬▬▬ 55

| 25 | MC GWIRE | 70 |
| 21 | SOSA | 66 |

Home Run Leaders

Rank	Player	Year	HR
1	Mark McGwire	1998	70
2	Sammy Sosa	1998	66
3	Roger Maris	1961	61
4	Babe Ruth	1927	60
5	Babe Ruth	1921	59

MARK SETS THE RECORD!

On September 7, 1998, Mark hit his 61st home run of the season. This was one more than Babe Ruth had hit in 1927. It also tied the record that Roger Maris had set in 1961. On September 8, 1998, Mark broke Roger Maris's record by hitting home run number 62. This was more than anyone had ever hit in one season! Sammy hit his 62nd home run five days later. It was a close race. Sammy was the first to hit 66, but Mark hit five more in his last three games. In fact, Mark hit his 70th home run on the last day of the season. He set the new record, and Sammy held second place with 66 home runs. Both players had fun in their home run race and they became good friends.

◀ *Mark and Sammy hugged after Mark hit his 62nd home run.*

THE HOME RUN KING

Mark is one of the most popular players in baseball today. Fans love to come early to the games so that they can see him practice hitting the ball. People also like Mark because he is a good person. Mark cares so much about children that he started something called the Mark McGwire Foundation for Children. This foundation helps protect children against **child abuse**. On top of all that, Mark is one of the best hitters baseball has ever seen. In 1999, he hit his 500th career home run against the San Diego Padres. Fans have always liked to see Mark play, but now he gets extra attention because he is the "Home Run King."

GLOSSARY

bases (BAY-siz) Four white, square bags a runner must step on to score a home run in baseball.

child abuse (CHYLD uh-BYOOS) When a child is treated roughly or cruelly.

college (KOL-ihj) A school you can go to after high school.

major leagues (MAY-jur LEEGZ) A group of the best baseball teams in North America.

minor league (MY-nuhr LEEG) A group of teams on which players play before they are good enough for the major leagues.

outfield (OWT-feeld) A part of the baseball field far away from home plate.

pitcher (PICH-ur) The player who throws the ball to batters on the other team and tries to get them out.

popular (POP-yoo-lur) Having many fans.

professional (proh-FESH-uh-nul) Someone who gets paid to play a sport.

record (REK-urd) When a player does something better than any other player ever has.

rookie (RUH-kee) A new major league player.

statistics (stuh-TIH-stix) Facts in the form of numbers.

swing (SWING) When a player tries to hit the baseball with his bat.

traded (TRAYD-ed) When a player has been given to another team in exchange for a player from that team.

World Series (WURLD SEER-ees) A group of games in which the two best baseball teams of the season play against each other.

INDEX

WEB SITES

To learn more about Mark McGwire and baseball, check out these Web sites:

http://mcgwire.kids.yahoo.com
http://www.mlb.com